Test# 110610
R.L.   6.7
Pts.   1.0

Washington Ablaze: The War of 1812

By Randy Schultz

Content Advisor:
Richard J. Bell
History Department
Harvard University

Rourke
Publishing LLC
Vero Beach, Florida 32964

www.rourkepublishing.com

Image Credits:
Library of Congress, cover (top left and right, bottom right), 1, 4, 6, 8–9,10, 12–13, 14, 15, 16, 17, 18, 19, 20, 21, 23, 28, 29, 32, 36, 37 (top), 38, 41, 42, 43, 44, 45 (top and bottom), 46 (first column and first three in second column); National Archives' Treasures of Congress, 40, 46 (second column bottom); iStockphoto, 5; Stock Montage, 24, 26, 30, 31, 45 (second from top); The Flag House & Star-Spangled Banner Museum, 34 (bottom right); Phil Martin Photography, 33, 34 (top, The Flag House & Star-Spangled Banner Museum), 35, 37

Editorial Direction: Red Line Editorial, Inc.; Bob Temple

Editor: Nadia Higgins

Designer: Lindaanne Donohoe

Fact Research: Laurie Kahn

Library of Congress Cataloging-in-Publication Data

Schultz, Randy.
  Washington ablaze : War of 1812 / Randy Schultz.
    p. cm. — (Events in American history)
  Includes bibliographical references and index.
    ISBN 1–60044–137–8 (hardcover)
    ISBN 978-1-60044-359-6 (paperback)
  1. United States—History—War of 1812—Juvenile literature. 2. Washington (D.C.)—History—Capture by the British, 1814– Juvenile literature. I. Title.
    E354.S47 2007
    973.5'2—dc22
                                2006018724

Printed in the USA

Rourke
Publishing LLC
Vero Beach, Florida 32964

Table of Contents

Chapter One

The Burning of Washington

On the morning of August 19, 1814, more than four thousand British troops arrived in Benedict, Maryland, near Washington, D.C. There was only one thing on the British leaders' minds: Head toward the capital of the United States and capture it.

"The ultimate destination of the [British] force was Washington, should it be found that the attempt might be made with any prospect of success."

British admiral George Cockburn, September 1814

Dolley Madison

First Lady Dolley Madison, wife of President James Madison, is remembered as a hero in her own right. During the War of 1812, she saved valuable papers and two national treasures.

As the British approached Washington, Dolley ran around the President's House collecting state papers, including the original copy of the Declaration of Independence. She also saved a famous picture of George Washington painted by Gilbert Stuart. Dolley was in such a hurry to save the painting she had the frame broken and the canvas taken out. Then she fled Washington in a carriage loaded with the rescued items. She returned to the city three days later. "I cannot tell you what I felt upon re-entering it," she wrote. "Such destruction—such confusion!"

Dolley Madison later wrote that, if the decision had been hers, she would have stayed to defend Washington. "If I could have had a cannon through every window, but alas! Those who should have placed them there fled before me, and my whole heart mourned for my country!"

Dolley Madison

Many battles had already been fought during the War of 1812. In one, Americans had attacked the capital city of Upper Canada (present-day Ontario), which was controlled by the British at the time. The British wanted revenge. Also, it had been only 38 years since the United States had won its independence from Great Britain during the Revolutionary War. Now the British were determined to get back what they thought was rightfully theirs.

British general Robert Ross could have led his men to Annapolis or Baltimore, Maryland's important port cities. Capturing either of those would have been a major victory. But the British felt that attacking the capital, even though it had fewer than eight thousand people, would damage the spirit of the young nation.

Even as British troops marched north from Benedict, the Americans were not sure of their destination. Soon enough, however, it became clear that the British were heading for the capital. As temperatures soared, American troops gathered on Maryland's Bladensburg Bridge to face the advancing British army. They were far outnumbered by the British.

> "I could not but admire the handsome manner in which the British officers led on their fatigued and worn-out soldiers."
>
> Charles Ball, an American soldier under the command of Joshua Barney

General Ross signaled his troops to storm the bridge. The American soldiers began scattering immediately. However, others farther up the road stood their ground. Under the command of Joshua Barney, they shot rounds of fire on the British. But the efforts of Barney's men were not enough. In this crucial battle, the Americans were badly defeated. Even Barney was wounded and taken prisoner.

The British pushed on toward Washington.

They stormed the U.S. capital and began setting it on fire. The nation's leaders, including President James Madison, had fled the city. The President's House, as the White House was called, was left empty for attack.

The escape from the President's House had been so hasty, a hot dinner for 40 people was left untouched on a dining-room table. When the British soldiers arrived, they feasted on the president's food and wine. Then they burned down the building.

By August 25, several other Washington, D.C., landmarks (including the House of Representatives and the Library of Congress) lay in charred ruins.

An illustration from 1814 shows Washington, D.C. on fire. British general Robert Ross is commanding his troops in the upper right corner.

"Few thought to go to bed—
they spent the night in gazing
on the fires and lamenting
the disgrace of the city."

*Mary Hunter,
a resident of Washington, D.C.*

The British claimed victory—and with that came one of the darkest moments in the young nation's history.

Chapter Two

Causes of War

In many ways, the War of 1812 began with another war. In the early 1800s, war raged between England and France. This war in Europe was having a disastrous effect on the United States. The young nation did not want to get involved in a conflict between foreign countries, but staying out of war was becoming more and more difficult.

At the time, England and France were far more powerful than the United States. These two mighty countries were passing laws affecting control of seaports. Their laws were mostly meant to hurt each other, but England and France didn't mind using neutral countries to advance their causes.

"I feel assured that no American will hesitate to rally round the standard of his insulted country in defense of that freedom and independence achieved by the wisdom of sages and consecrated by the blood of heroes."
Thomas Jefferson, 1809

Opposite page: A political cartoon shows Napoleon Bonaparte, France's ruler in the early 1800s, throwing a fit over his country's problems with Great Britain.

First, France closed all ports in mainland Europe to the British. The British, in turn, developed a plan that forced any neutral ship—such as an American one—to stop in Great Britain before heading to other European ports. The neutral ship was to pay a duty, or tax, on its cargo. Any ship that didn't follow these orders would be captured by the British. In response to this, the French then said they would seize any ship entering or leaving a British port.

The United States depended heavily on commerce with both countries. The laws were making it more and more difficult for U.S. trade ships to go about their business. American shipbuilders and merchants were losing money.

Massachusett's Boston Harbor was a key U.S. port in the early 1800s.

The United States was angry with both England and France because of their policies at sea. However, England enforced another practice, called impressment, that enraged Americans even more. British military ships were stopping American trade ships at sea. The British then forced American sailors to come and work on the British ships. The British said they were just taking back British sailors who had deserted, or illegally left, their navy. This may have been the case sometimes, but the British weren't careful about whom they took. They often ended up capturing American-born sailors. In the eyes of the United States, the British were kidnapping American sailors. This was a huge blow to the pride of the young country.

In June of 1807, the issue of impressment came to a head. For the first time, the British stopped a U.S. navy ship instead of a trade ship. The British military ship *Leopard* stopped the USS *Chesapeake* in American waters. The British demanded to be let on board the *Chesapeake* to search for British sailors. When the Americans refused, the British attacked. The British took four sailors from the *Chesapeake* and killed one of them. For a time, war looked likely.

"[Great Britain's] claim of right was to take by force all sea-faring men, her own subjects, wherever they were found by her naval officers, to serve their king in his wars. And under color of this tyrant's right, her naval officers, down to the most beardless midshipman, actually took from the American merchant vessels which they visited, any seaman whom they chose to take for a British subject.

John Quincy Adams (U.S. president, 1825–29) in "The Origin of the War" (1812), describing the British practice of impressment

A cartoon from 1813 shows Britain's point of view on the takeover of the USS Chesapeake. The Americans are depicted as fools.

Thomas Jefferson

President Thomas Jefferson looked for a peaceful solution —at least to the troubles with European trade. He pushed Congress to pass the Embargo Act in December 1807. This law closed all American ports to foreign ships and required American ships to sail only to U.S. ports. The idea was that completely cutting off trade with Europe would cause England and France to lose a lot of money. That would force them to end their policies, which were damaging U.S. trade.

The Embargo Act backfired. Shipbuilders and sailors in New England nearly went broke. Southern plantation owners also lost a market for their rice, tobacco, and cotton crops; the goods rotted in warehouses. In newspapers around the country, people were writing articles against the Embargo Act. They made fun of the act by calling it O-Grab-Me, which is *embargo* spelled backward.

"Be it enacted ... that an embargo be, and hereby is laid on all ships and vessels in the ports and places within the limits or jurisdiction of the United States, cleared or not cleared, bound to any foreign port or place; and that no clearance be furnished to any ship or vessel bound to such foreign port or place, except vessels under the immediate direction of the President of the United States."

The Embargo Act of 1807

African American slaves pick cotton on a Southern plantation. After the Embargo Act, plantation owners could not sell their crops to foreign markets, and business suffered.

A cartoon from 1808 shows Thomas Jefferson (behind the desk) defending the Embargo Act to a group of unhappy citizens. One man responds, "My family is starving."

The Embargo Act lasted 14 months. Over the next few years, Congress tried modified solutions, but none of them had the effect the Americans hoped for. Finally, in 1810, the United States gave up all restrictions on trade. In addition, the government held out a deal to France and England: If England took back its laws, the United States would stop trading with France. On the other hand, if France took back its laws, then the United States would stop trading with England.

France saw an opportunity. It *pretended* to take back its earlier policies about neutral shipping. Americans stopped trade with England. Tensions between the two countries grew worse.

Chapter Three

The Country Debates

James Madison

James Madison had become president in 1809. Like Jefferson, he had tried to avoid war. By November of 1811, however, Madison was advising Congress to prepare for one.

Debate raged through Congress for several months. The country's leaders were deeply divided.

Those opposed to war generally came from New England, the northern states along the East Coast. More than any other area of the country, New England depended on overseas trade. A war with Great Britain— the most powerful country on the sea—could wipe out New England's economy. Also, many New Englanders sympathized with the British and their struggle with France.

"The present situation of the world is indeed without a parallel, and that of our own country full of difficulties. The pressure of these, too, is the more severely felt because they have fallen upon us at a moment when the national prosperity being at a height not before attained, the contrast resulting from the change has been rendered the more striking."

James Madison in his first speech as president, March 4, 1809

William Henry Harrison

It was because of his reputation as an Indian fighter and military hero during the War of 1812 that William Henry Harrison was elected president of the United States in 1840.

In 1811, Harrison led a thousand soldiers into battle against American Indians on the Tippecanoe River. The Indians drew back after the brief and bloody battle, after which their village was burned down by Harrison's troops.

While the battle was considered a victory by the Americans, it led to more Indian raids. It also led to the Indians' siding with the British in the War of 1812.

During the War of 1812, Harrison led American troops to victory in the Battle of the Thames but resigned from the military a short time later. He pursued his political career and was eventually elected president in 1840.

Harrison became ill almost as soon as his term in office began. He died after just one month of service as the ninth president of the United States.

William Henry Harrison

In the House of Representatives, congressmen in favor of war were known as War Hawks. These men were from the western and southern states, and they held powerful positions in Congress. Two leaders of this group were Speaker of the House of Representatives Henry Clay of Kentucky and John C. Calhoun of South Carolina.

The War Hawks felt the country's pride was at stake. Some also saw war as an opportunity for the country to gain land. The 13 colonies had fought for their independence from British rule during the Revolutionary War. But, to the north, Canada was still under British control. Land-hungry Americans hoped to push the British out of Canada and expand U.S. territories.

Right: Henry Clay
Below: John C. Calhoun

"In the Eastern States the opposition to the war was marked and virulent. ... In the Middle and Southern States, public opinion was divided, [though] a large majority approved the measures adopted by Congress. But in the West there was only one sentiment: love of country sparkled in every eye, and animated every heart."

John Quincy Adams
(U.S. president, 1825–29)
in "The Origin of the War," (1812)

Americans along the country's northwest border also saw the British as an obstacle to pushing west. Settlers moving into Ohio and the Indiana Territory had encountered a lot of resistance from the American Indians living there. Americans believed the British were helping the Indians, maybe even supplying them with guns.

"Be it enacted ... that war be and the same is hereby declared to exist between the United Kingdom of Great Britain ... and the United States of America ... and that the President of the United States is hereby authorized to use the whole land and naval force of the United States to carry the same into effect."

U.S. Declaration of War, 1812

Then, in November 1811, American soldiers were attacked by Indians in the Battle of Tippecanoe near present-day Lafayette, Indiana. Following the battle, British guns were found on the battlefield.

In their quest for land, many Americans looked south as well. They had an eye on Florida, which was ruled by Spain at the time—and Spain was an ally of Great Britain.

In the end, the War Hawks brought President Madison to their side. On June 1, 1812, Madison asked Congress to declare war on Great Britain. The main reasons he gave were Great Britain's impressment of American seamen, its interference with U.S. trade, and its support of Indian warfare in the northwest.

Congress did declare war several weeks later. The vote in the House of Representatives was 79 in favor and 49 against. In the Senate, it was 19 in favor and 13 against.

Little did the Americans know that just two days earlier, Great Britain had taken back the laws that had been the original cause of trouble. In 1812, news traveled slowly. It came in letters carried by boats and horse-drawn vehicles. Word of this announcement didn't arrive in the United States until it was too late. The war was already on.

This 1889 painting shows American soldiers firing at Indians during the Battle of Tippecanoe, November 1811.

Chapter Four

War Is Here

The War of 1812 would last nearly three years. In that time, more than 60 battles took place on land and sea. Each side had its share of victories. Often, there was no clear winner or loser.

Congress had known for seven months that war was coming. Even so, no real preparations were made. The treasury had little money. Worse yet, the army had fewer than ten thousand troops—and not enough officers to lead them. The navy had fewer than 20 ships available.

"I feel it my duty to state that the conduct of Captain Hull [of the *Constitution*] and his officers to our men has been that of a brave enemy, the greatest care being taken to prevent our men losing the smallest trifle, and the greatest attention being paid to the wounded."

James Richard Dacres, captain of the defeated Guerrière, in a report back to Great Britain

"As the war was just in its origin and necessary and noble in its objects, we can reflect with a proud satisfaction that in carrying it on no principle of justice or honor, no usage of civilized nations, no precept of courtesy or humanity, have been infringed. The war has been waged on our part with scrupulous regard to all these obligations, and in a spirit of liberality which was never surpassed."

President James Madison, in a speech taking on his second term of office, March 4, 1813

Nevertheless, many Americans believed victory would be easy. After all, many British soldiers were still tied up in a war against France.

The U.S. strategy was to attack British-held Canada. American troops marched north to the border but were soon pushed back. In Detroit, they faced not only British troops but Indian fighters under the command of their leader, Tecumseh. American general William Hull quickly surrendered. The defeat was such an embarrassment for Americans that Hull was later

sentenced to death for his conduct during the battle. The ruling was overturned, however.

In 1812 and 1813, the Americans continued to try to invade Canada, but they were not successful. At one point, U.S. troops did manage to capture York (present-day Toronto), the capital of Upper Canada. They burned government buildings and held the city for a short time. By December 1813, however, the British had the upper hand. They crossed into western New York and burned Buffalo and nearby towns.

The wife of an American soldier is shown on the front lines of the battle to defend Fort Niagara, in western New York.

Old Ironsides

Old Ironsides, or the USS *Constitution*, was one of the U.S. Navy's very first ships. Built in Boston between 1794 and 1797, the 204-foot-long (62 meters) *Constitution* was fitted for five hundred crewmembers. The ship was a 44-gun frigate, which meant it was built to hold 44 cannons of various sizes, but she often carried more. Old Ironsides had 72 canvas sails. With favorable winds, she could sail along at 14 knots (15 miles or 24 kilometers per hour).

The battle with *Guerrière* was Old Ironside's most famous moment, but it went on to other successes at sea. In 1830, when the worn-out ship was ordered to be destroyed, Oliver Wendell Holmes paid tribute to it in a poem. "The meteor of the ocean air / Shall sweep the clouds no more," he wrote.

People were so moved by the poem, the ship was rebuilt and put back into service. It was repaired again in 1877 and 1930. Today, Old Ironsides floats in Boston Harbor and can be toured by visitors.

The USS Constitution, *known as Old Ironsides*

Early on, the U.S. had more success at sea, which was astonishing given that the fledgling U.S. Navy was fighting the most powerful naval force in the world. One of the most famous battles of the war took place between the American ship *Constitution* and the British *Guerrière*. On August 19, 1812, the two ships met off the coast of Canada. The British started firing right away. The Americans held their fire as cannonballs bounced off the sides of the *Constitution's* oak hull. Seeing this, one crewmember supposedly declared, "Hurrah, her sides are made of iron!" This remark led to the ship's nickname, Old Ironsides, by which it is famously known.

When the British ship came close, American captain Isaac Hull (the nephew of William Hull) gave his crew the orders to fire. The *Guerrière* went down fast. The American victory at sea was not strategically important but boosted the spirit of the country. Hull became a hero, and the New England states began to rally in support of the war.

American soldiers defended the Constitution *during what would become one of the war's most famous battles.*

By summer of 1813, however, the memory of the *Constitution*'s victory was fading. British ships had U.S. ports surrounded. The blockade devastated American trade. Once again, crops piled up in warehouses and businesses suffered.

Then on September 10, Oliver Hazard Perry led a stunning American victory on Lake Erie. After the battle he wrote his famous message to General William Henry Harrison: "We have met the enemy, and they are ours."

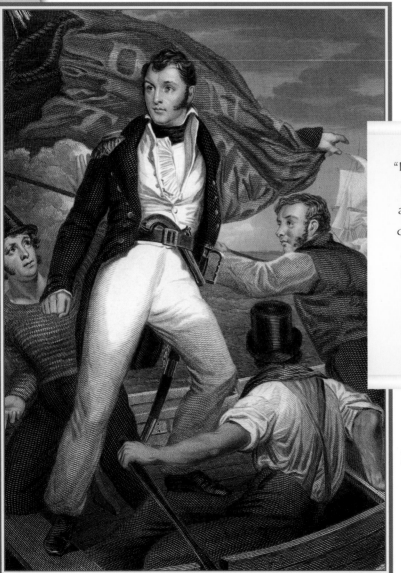

"It has pleased the Almighty to give to the arms of the United States a signal victory over their enemies on this lake. The British squadron … have this moment surrendered to the force under my command, after a sharp conflict."

Oliver Hazard Perry, in a report about the Battle of Lake Erie

Oliver Hazard Perry

After the Battle of Lake Erie, British troops fled Detroit. General Harrison and his men chased the British north into Canada. The two sides finally came to battle at Ontario's Thames River on October 5. Joining the British were Tecumseh and six hundred Indian soldiers. After the first round of shots, many of the British fled, leaving the Indians to face the Americans alone. Tecumseh was killed in battle, and the alliance between the British and the Indians ended.

In this painting, Tecumseh is shot point blank by an American soldier during the Battle of the Thames. Though probably not historically accurate, the painting captures the dramatic impact of the Indian leader's death.

Chapter Five

Battles of 1814

By 1814, Britain's war with France had ended. The European power could now focus all of its attention on the United States. Boatloads of troops landed on American shores, doubling Britain's forces in the war.

Suddenly, prospects for an American victory seemed dim. Would the United States become British colonies once again?

When the British burned Washington, D.C., in August, spirits sank even further, but the tide was about to turn. After their victory in the nation's capital, British troops headed toward Baltimore, Maryland. Baltimore was the third-largest U.S. city and an important harbor. Losing this commercial center would be a huge blow to the Americans.

Opposite page: Fort McHenry, Baltimore, was the site of a key battle in the War of 1812.
Below: A plaque at Fort McHenry dedicates a tree to a soldier killed in battle at the fort.

"We should have to fight hereafter not for 'free Trade and sailors rights,' not for the Conquest of the Canadas, but for our national Existence."

Congressman Joseph H. Nicholson of Maryland to the Secretary of the Navy, May 1814

Above: Mary Young Pickersgill and her daughter, Caroline, sewed Fort McHenry's enormous flag by hand. Right: The only known photo of Mary Pickersgill

Unlike Washington, however, Baltimore was ready for the British. Every white male between the ages of 16 and 50 was drafted for battle. The citizens of the city pitched in to dig trenches and get cannons ready. Mary Young Pickersgill and her 13-year-old daughter, Caroline, sewed a giant U.S. flag in a brewery (a place where beer is made). Supposedly, it was the only local building with enough space for them to spread out the great amount of cloth. The women stayed at the brewery into the night, sewing by candlelight. The huge flag was of utmost importance. It would fly above Fort McHenry, which guarded the city's harbor. Its enormous size would let the approaching British know that the Americans were not afraid.

A plaque at Fort McHenry pays tribute to Francis Scott Key, who wrote the words to what became "The Star-Spangled Banner."

"We are in a deplorable situation ... our commerce dead; our revenue gone; our ships rotting on the wharves.... Our treasury drained—we are bankrupts."

Massachusetts politician Daniel Sargent, in a speech to the Massachusetts General Assembly, fall 1814

The British arrived in Baltimore on September 12, 1814. The following morning, British ships began firing on Fort McHenry. They fired into the night.

An American lawyer, Francis Scott Key, happened to be on a ship in the harbor that night. He was in Baltimore to arrange for the release of an American doctor who had been taken prisoner. When he arrived for talks with the British, he didn't expect to become a witness to one of the most important battles of the war.

"The Star-Spangled Banner"

Francis Scott Key did not set out to write a song, never mind a national anthem. His poem "The Defense of Fort McHenry" was published in a flyer shortly after Key finished it in Baltimore. It was so popular that a newspaper reprinted the poem under a new title, "The Star-Spangled Banner." Soon people were singing the words to the tune of an old English song, "To Anacreon in Heaven." The song—with its new words—became more and more popular. In 1931, Congress declared "The Star-Spangled Banner" the country's national anthem.

Today, the first verse of the song is well-known:

O say, can you see, by the dawn's early light,

What so proudly we hail'd at the twilight's last gleaming?

Whose broad stripes and bright stars, thro' the perilous fight,

O'er the ramparts we watch'd, were so gallantly streaming?

And the rockets' red glare, the bombs bursting in air,

Gave proof thro' the night that our flag was still there.

O say, does that star-spangled banner yet wave

O'er the land of the free and the home of the brave?

From a ship in Baltimore Harbor, Francis Scott Key watched the giant flag wave over Fort McHenry.

That night, a thunderstorm raged. As rain fell and lightning flashed around the fort, rockets and exploding mortars looked like fireworks in the black sky. The noise was deafening.

Amid the lights and noise, Key wondered what was happening. When daylight appeared the next morning, the huge flag, with 15 stars and stripes, was still flying over Fort McHenry. The city had not been taken.

Key was so inspired, he immediately scribbled a few lines of a poem on an envelope. Two days later, the full poem, "The Defense of Fort McHenry," was finished in Baltimore. Today his poem is better known as the lyrics to "The Star-Spangled Banner"—the American national anthem.

Right: A cover to sheet music of "The Star-Spangled Banner" from around 1860
Below: A cannon once stationed at Fort McHenry faces the Fracis Scott Key Bridge over the Baltimore Harbor.

Chapter Six

After the War

Who won the War of 1812? There was no clear winner. Instead, the two sides simply wore themselves out.

By the winter of 1814, both the Americans and the British wanted the conflict to end. British taxpayers were tired of paying for the war effort, and the Americans feared disaster if British troops remained on their land.

Opposite page: The Battle of New Orleans was fought after the War of 1812 had officially ended.

"It is highly honorable to our country to have maintained its ground, singly, against G. Britain, & to have forced her to such a peace. This contest has been glorious to the U States."

James Madison, in a letter from 1815

"Peace, at all times a blessing, is peculiarly welcome ... at a period when the causes for the war have ceased to operate, when the Government has demonstrated the efficiency of its powers of defense, and when the nation can review its conduct without regret and without reproach."

President James Madison, in a speech to Congress announcing the end of the war, February 18, 1815

> "There shall be a firm and universal peace between His Britannic Majesty and the United States, and between their respective countries, territories, cities, towns, and people, of every degree, without exception of places or persons. All hostilities, both by sea and land, shall cease as soon as this treaty shall have been ratified by both parties."
>
> *Treaty of Ghent, signed December 24, 1814*

The Treaty of Ghent

The two sides met in Belgium and on December 24 signed the Treaty of Ghent, officially ending the War of 1812. The treaty didn't address any of the reasons why the United States had gone to war in the first place. For example, no mention was made of the British impressment of American sailors or Britain's other policies at sea. However, the treaty did release all war prisoners. The United States had to return the land it had won in Canada. Britain had to return the land it had won as well. In other words, boundaries went back to the way they were before the war.

The treaty also ended the fighting—at least on paper. While news of the treaty slowly made its way from Belgium to the United States, British and American troops were gathering in New Orleans for a final, bloody battle. Unaware that the war was over, American troops, led by Andrew Jackson, overwhelmingly defeated the British on January 8, 1815. The British had 1,550 men killed or wounded, while only 14 Americans were killed and 39 wounded.

An 1842 illustration shows Andrew Jackson (on the white horse) leading Americans to victory at the Battle of New Orleans.

Andrew Jackson

Andrew Jackson came from a poor family in South Carolina. By the time Jackson was 14, he was an orphan.

Jackson was a general in the Tennessee militia when the War of 1812 broke out. He immediately offered his services to President Madison. He also organized a group of 2,500 Tennessee volunteers to fight in Canada.

Even before the Battle of New Orleans, Jackson had gained fame as a soldier. At one point, he led his men across 500 miles (805 kilometers) of wilderness in the southern parts of the United States. During the march, one of his men supposedly said that Jackson was "tough as hickory" (a hard wood). This earned Jackson his nickname, Old Hickory.

In March 1814, Jackson became known as an Indian fighter. He led American troops in a bloody victory against the Creek Indians of Alabama. As a result of that war, the United States gained vast portions of Creek land in what is now Georgia and Alabama.

Jackson's fame eventually led to his election as president of the United States in 1828. He served two terms, from 1829 to 1837.

Andrew Jackson, pictured after his victory over Creek Indians in 1814

News of the Treaty of Ghent reached the United States on February 11, 1815, but Americans did not show regret for the Battle of New Orleans. Rather, Andrew Jackson was hailed as a national hero.

The War of 1812 changed the United States in many ways. The war had forced Americans not to rely so heavily on trade with Great Britain and to learn to manufacture their own goods. So the production of American-made items increased tremendously.

The war led to increases in U.S. land. The Americans had occupied a part of Florida during the war. Afterward, the country was able to acquire of the rest of that territory from Spain. Also, with Tecumseh dead, the Indians had lost a lot of power in the northwest. The United States pushed westward, taking over Indian land along the way.

With the War of 1812, the young nation had proven itself. The American people had been severely tested and successfully showed their independence. The country united, and patriotism grew. The United States was on its way to becoming a world power.

Settlers with covered wagons cross the Great Plains.
The War of 1812 opened the West to U.S. citizens in search of fortune.

Biographies

William Henry Harrison (1773–1841)

William Henry Harrison was born in Virginia to a wealthy and influential family. His father was a friend of George Washington. Harrison became a military hero in 1811 after defeating American Indians at the Battle of Tippecanoe. As a result, Harrison's nickname became Tippecanoe. When Harrison took office in 1841, he caught a cold. A month later he died, becoming the first president to die in office.

Andrew Jackson (1767–1845)

Andrew Jackson was born in Waxhaw, South Carolina. His military career began when he was just 14, in a minor fight against the British in 1781. In 1788, Jackson moved to Tennessee, where he would work as a lawyer, politician, military general, and owner of a cotton plantation. During the War of 1812, Jackson led the American victory at the Battle of New Orleans, which made him a national hero. In 1828, Jackson was elected president of the United States and served two terms in office. He is credited with starting the Democratic political party.

Francis Scott Key (1779–1843)

Francis Scott Key was the Washington lawyer who, after witnessing the Battle of Baltimore in 1814, wrote a poem that would later become the words of the national anthem. He went on to write a book of poems, many of which were religious. Key was also an abolitionist, someone who worked to end the practice of slavery.

Dolley Madison (1768–1849)

Dolley Madison grew up in Virginia and Philadelphia. Her parents were members of the Quaker religion, known for its strong antiwar beliefs. When she was 22, she married John Todd and they had two sons. In 1793, Dolley's husband and younger son died. The next year, she married James Madison, who was then a congressman. Because James was not a Quaker, Dolley was kicked out of her religion. Dolley Madison is famous for saving valuable state papers during the attack on Washington, D.C., in 1814. She is also remembered as a warm and generous hostess.

James Madison (1751–1836)

Born in Virginia, James Madison was the oldest of 12 children. He was often sick growing up. At 23, he entered local politics in Virginia and devoted the next 40 years of his life to public service. Madison was the fourth president of the United States, serving from 1809 to 1817. Before that, he played a leading role in drafting the U.S. Constitution, the document that outlines the country's most basic laws.

Oliver Hazard Perry (1785–1819)

Perry led the American naval fleet that beat the British in the Battle of Lake Erie on September 10, 1813. A few hours into the battle, Perry had to leave the ship he was commanding. With British fire blasting all around him, he rowed in a small boat to another ship, the *Niagara*. Shortly after Perry took command of the *Niagara*, the six British ships surrendered. That was the first time in history that an entire British naval fleet had done so.

Tecumseh (ca. 1768–1813)

Before siding with the British in the War of 1812, Tecumseh worked to form a union of American Indian tribes in the northeastern parts of the United States. He believed that together, the tribes could push back the white settlers who were taking over Indian lands. After Tecumseh's death at the Battle of the Thames in 1813, the dream of a united Indian front fell apart. Tecumseh is remembered as a brave warrior and gifted speaker. Even William Henry Harrison, his enemy on the battlefield, called him "one of those uncommon geniuses which spring up occasionally to produce revolutions and overturn the established order of things."

Timeline

June 22, 1807
The British ship *Leopard* attacks the USS *Chesapeake*.

1807

December 1807
Congress passes the Embargo Act; U.S. trade soon comes to a halt.

June 18, 1812
The United States declares war on Great Britain.

August 19, 1812
USS *Constitution* defeats HMS *Guerrière* and earns the nickname Old Ironsides.

September 10, 1813
Oliver Hazard Perry leads United States to victory at Lake Erie.

August 24, 1814
The British burn the President's House and other important buildings in Washington, D.C.

September 13–14, 1814
Americans successfully defend Fort McHenry; Francis Scott Key writes words of future national anthem.

December 24, 1814
The Treaty of Ghent, officially ending the war, is signed in Belgium.

January 8, 1815
Andrew Jackson leads an American victory in New Orleans at what has been called the Needless Battle.

1815

Glossary

anthem (AN-thum)
an uplifting song meant to inspire a country or a cause

blockade (blok-AYD)
the act of surrounding a place, such as a port, in order to control which goods or people can enter or leave it

colony (KOL-uh-nee)
a group of people who settle in a distant land while remaining citizens of their own country; also the word for the place they settle

desert (dih-ZURT)
to quit military service without permission

draft (DRAFT)
to legally force a person meeting certain conditions to serve in the military

duty (DOO-tee)
payment collected by the government, often added to the price of goods

embargo (ehm-BAR-go)
a government order that stops trade ships from doing business at its country's ports

impressment (im-PREHS-mehnt)
the practice of forcing people to serve in the military

manufacture (MAN-u-FAK-chur)
to make items, usually by machine, and often at factories

militia (muh-LISH-uh)
a group of nonprofessional, citizen soldiers organized for an emergency

neutral (NOO-truhl)
not supporting either side in a war or disagreement

Further Resources

Web Links

HistoryCentral.com: The War of 1812
www.historycentral.com/1812/Index.html
This site offers a short description of all major battles in the War of 1812. Includes historical maps and illustrations.

National Park Service: Fort McHenry
www.nps.gov/fomc
This site offers in-depth information on the fort, the Battle of Baltimore, and "The Star-Spangled Banner."

The War of 1812 Website
www.warof1812.ca

In addition to articles and images, this site includes sound clips, animated battle maps, and quizzes about the War of 1812.

Books

Crewe, Sabrina, and Scott Ingram. *The Writing of "The Star-Spangled Banner."* Gareth Stevens, 2005.

Santella, Andrew. *The War of 1812.* Children's Press, 2001.

Smalley, Roger. *Dolley Madison Saves History.* Capstone Press, 2006.

Index